The Boss Behind The Boss

Secretarial Success
Secrets Revealed!

Lynne Tunis Parlier

All rights reserved under United States and International Copyright Conventions

2nd Edition
Copyright © 2017 by Lynne Tunis Parlier
No part of this book may be reproduced or utilized in any form or by any means, electronic or mechanical, including photocopying, recording or by any information storage and retrieval system, without permission in writing from the author.

ISBN: 1545418284
ISBN 13: 9781545418284

Table of Contents

FOREWORD ...A brief explanation		v
1	A VIEW FROM THE TOP	1
	...What makes a good secretary / administrative assistant (AA)?	1
	...What would make them *BETTER*?	1
2	STARTING THE DAY ...Are you BOTH prepared for it?	7
3	*YOU* ARE THE COMPANY ...Front door to the business	10
4	SCHEDULES & CALENDAR MANAGEMENT ...Vying for precious time!	15
5	FILES ...Not necessarily drudgery	20
6	CRISIS MANAGEMENT ...Murphy's Law & *YOU*!	25
7	IS IT LUNCHTIME ALREADY? ...From popcorn to paté	29
8	MINUTES, MEETINGS & ICE CREAM ...Again, *planning*	33
9	BIRTHDAYS, BALLOONS & THANK YOUs ...*YOU* are his memory!	38
10	GETTING & BUILDING SUPPORT ...Up, down & across	45

11	ARE DESKTOP COMPUTERS OBSOLETE? ...Technology tools are changing!	49
12	COMMUNICATING WITH YOUR BOSS ...Sometimes *not* so easy	53
13	WHEN HE'S READY TO GO HOME ...Avoiding late night calls!	59
14	THE DREADED MOVING DAY ...Across the hall or across town	63
15	BEING PROFESSIONAL ...Not a myth, but *YOUR* career!	70
16	ODDS & ENDS ...Other situations that arise ...Working with an EA	74
17	"WE'VE COME A LONG WAY, BABY" ...Past, Present and Future	83
	About the author...	85

Foreword

...A brief explanation

THIS IS *NOT* a book on how to become, or be, a secretary or administrative assistant (AA), but rather how to become a *better* one. The author takes a bit of an old-fashioned view that "My job is to make your (the boss's) job easier." Using this premise, *The Boss Behind The Boss* is filled with helpful hints to aid you in your job. The rewards of using this book can lead to personal enrichment, higher pay and possible promotion. Use the hints and suggestions applicable to *you* and *your* job situations. They worked for me and many others from the feedback I've received from my first edition of this book.

Although this book applies to both male and female secretaries and/or AAs and their male or female bosses, the author will refer to the boss as "he" or "him" and to the secretary as "she" or "her" to facilitate reading and understanding. Please accept the author's license for using a "traditional" model. No offense or discrimination is intended.

Throughout this book, many chapters will utilize a short sentence or narrative paragraph for both conciseness and ease in remembering important points. You also may find the subject matter may more readily adapt to your own individual checklist format of dashes or bullet points. Book formatting prevented this.

The author had thirty years of secretarial experience in the corporate business world, from a secretarial neophyte business intern in high school to becoming a seasoned executive secretary with one of America's largest telecommunications corporation. Although secretarial titles change as the roles and levels of responsibility evolve, the basic job function of supporting the boss remains relatively the same in today's fast paced competitive business world, but now using increased complex technological skills.

As a secretary, or administrative assistant, you are the other half of an important duo and the reputation you help craft reflects on both you and your boss. Improving your job skills will enhance both parties and the perception of a professional "team" will become self-evident as you apply the principles and suggestions in this book. Remember, truly *YOU* are *The Boss Behind The Boss*!

The author wishes to acknowledge and thank her husband, David, who encouraged her to be creative and put her career thoughts on paper to share with others.

1
A View from the Top

...What makes a good secretary / administrative assistant (AA)?

...What would make them *BETTER*?

MANY COMPANY OWNERS, corporate executives and managers were surveyed and asked "what qualities make a good secretary or administrative assistant?" and "what qualities or skills would make them *better*?" The following responses are in no particular order of importance.

"A good secretary or administrative assistant (AA)...

- ...is one who anticipates my needs, even before I do
- ...is dependable, truly dependable
- ...works hard at making my job easier
- ...knows everyone and their function under my supervision
- ...knows who to contact to get things done
- ...keeps me organized

...makes the mechanics of my job transparent to the job function
...is professional at all times
...is confident of her position and abilities
...makes me dread when she's out sick or on vacation
...is one of my strongest assets at work
...manages people well to get things done
...is loyal
...is discreet about her and my jobs, when required
...doesn't gossip with others
...dresses, looks and acts professional
...keeps away those I don't want to see and makes sure I see those I want to
...doesn't need a lot of direction
...knows my strengths as well as my weaknesses
...is in control
...knows me inside and out
...makes me feel at ease
...can make or break relationships with our customers
...diffuses angry customers or employees
...knows how to delegate work, when needed
...commands respect from those who work with her
...is motivated and a self-starter
...knows the office politics, but avoids them
...balances my workload and my workday
...is invaluable
...probably doesn't get enough thanks from me
...is the front door to my office
...is available when needed
...is hard to find and keep

...works for me first and then others when she has time
...knows her job well
...can sometimes anticipate and solve problems before they get to me
...is an integral part of my management team
...takes an interest in my projects
...guides me through the day
...is always improving her skills
...has a passion for excellence
...is my 'inside' salesperson
...is pleasant even when having a bad day
...takes initiative and makes things happen
...suggests improvements for mutual job efficiencies
...communicates openly with me and will talk through our differences
...isn't afraid to tackle anything
...asks for help if she doesn't understand something
...makes our customers feel important
...is my memory bank, helping me to remember not only business dates, but birthdays, anniversaries and other important events
...makes *me* look good
...is the pulse of my organization
...makes meetings run smoothly
...is cheerful on the telephone and in the office
...screens less important calls
...loves her work and shows it
...effectively utilizes her support organizations
...knows how to 'network' effectively

...builds support for me at all levels
...is always punctual, if not early
...should remain a secretary if that's her career path
...protects my flank at all times."

"What would make them *BETTER*?"
When asked "what would make your secretary, or AA, *BETTER*?", these same owners, executives and managers replied...

"I wish she (or he) would...

...anticipate problems sooner so that a crisis could be avoided
...be more interested in the business
...take more initiative
...learn the product lines in order to be able to talk about the business with callers and clients
...come to me early on when something is bothering her
...be more enthusiastic and competitive
...avail herself of more training and self-development
...keep me better informed
...be more discreet about my business
...not wait to be asked for something
...be more professional
...improve her vocabulary
...develop better computer skills
...keep personal business or personal telephone calls at work to a minimum
...not be afraid to make mistakes or ask questions

- ...present me with options, e.g. travel arrangements, meeting times, etc.
- ...be more flexible with office hours and overtime
- ...develop a team approach relationship with me versus a superior/subordinate one.
- ...stand up for her convictions if she's right and I'm wrong
- ...be more aggressive
- ...be a team player
- ...better organize herself and me
- ...learn what's really important, as well as unimportant, to me
- ...discuss her career plans with me
- ...be punctual
- ...take on more responsibility
- ...keep apprising me of due dates, important events, etc.
- ...have contingency plans for critical events. (Plans A and B)
- ...avoid gossip and the company grapevine
- ...not assume that I know everything that's going on
- ...tell me when the workload may require additional help
- ...properly train temporary help before vacations, leaves or training
- ...not leave me stranded with anything
- ...sensitize me to others' views
- ...not let me take her for granted
- ...give me a little too much information rather than not enough

...be able to communicate up and down the organization
...be a 'go-getter'
...take criticism constructively
...not hide important feelings from me."

2
Starting the Day

...Are you BOTH prepared for it?
SOME SAY BREAKFAST is the most important meal of the day. Many secretaries and AAs will agree that the first hour of the workday may determine how the rest of the day will go. The real estate axiom of "Location, location, location" can be rivaled with the secretarial axiom of "Preparation, preparation, preparation." Take a few minutes to organize your day and the rewards will be smoother hours ahead. You are organizing not only yourself, but also the boss. A suggested checklist should include the following:

Organize yourself first. Check your own work folder to see what you have to do that day.

Also check "Awaiting Responses" folder, "Bring-Up" folder and/or "Tickle" file for information/action due today.

Unload the boss's briefcase, if appropriate, to see what mail was handled the night before and is now ready for further processing (See Chapter 13 - "When He's Ready To Go Home" for details)

Review his daily smart phone planner or schedule card (a 3"x5" card which includes his meeting schedule, meeting location, attendees, topic of meeting and duration). See Chapter 13. Other important events should be highlighted.

Check with the boss to see if he has changed the schedule without letting you know. Bosses are both famous and infamous for this.

Make sure the boss has all meeting materials including backup matter requiring any additional preparation by you or a technical assistant.

Are there open items from the previous day which need additional information or action in order to be resolved?

An organized work area sets the tone of the day. Efficient desk set-up (both his and yours) should include pencils sharpened, pens in writing condition, calendar opened, pad to write down anything he asks you to do, etc.

I personally didn't mind getting coffee, tea or other refreshments for my boss throughout his busy day. Many secretaries or assistants do not see this as part of their job and should resolve this issue, either way, with their boss early in the game.

Double-check his luncheon plans to make sure there are no surprises such as time changes, extra guests, restaurant changes or even cancellations.

Apprise the receptionist (if it is not you) of any calls he wishes to receive or be handled differently. However, the disposition of most of his calls will go through you.

Check both his and your telephone sets to confirm they're operational and not on call forwarding or other programmed features on your PBX or key telephone system. Bosses have a funny way of messing with their telephones when you are not around to show them how to use a feature.

Check with the message center (if applicable) or answering machine for any previous messages from yesterday which may have come in after you left.

Check for adequate paper in the copy machine and other general office supplies. Morning may be an excellent time to place an order with the office supply store or get them from your internal supply room.

Check the fax machine for adequate paper. Pick up the handset and check for dial tone to make sure it's working. Assemble incoming faxes for distribution or copies.

For security from prying eyes, some fax machines may contain buffer memories which can store messages without printing until a security code is punched in for access. Don't forget to check this feature if your system has it. You may want to mention this feature to your boss if there is sensitivity about secure fax communications.

Reconfirm meetings early in the day that were confirmed the day before with those whom your boss is to visit or to receive. Not everyone is as organized as, hopefully, you are and may have forgotten the appointment entirely or have the wrong time planned.

Take a few moments to evaluate the boss's attitude when he first comes in so you can adjust your actions and reactions accordingly. A bad night, a family emergency or late night business calls can affect his attitude for the rest of the day.

3
You are the Company

...Front door to the business

THE FOLLOWING SECTION deals with successful telephone techniques, the art of screening calls (if desired), handling referrals and getting resolution over the phone.

Know the boss's preference for the way the telephone is to be answered, how calls are to be screened, or referred, and who does and doesn't get through to him.

Don't be too quick to give out too much information. The boss's and the company's business is not everyone's business.

Learn to use the telephone system you have correctly. Reread the manual or contact the vendor for training. Nothing is worse than to tell the calling party you will give him another number to call "...in case I lose you while I am transferring you".

Identify yourself on the phone. "Good morning. Mr. Smith's office. Ms. Jones speaking" or "John Smith's office, how may I help you?"

Don't ask "Who is this?" There are nicer ways to get the information like "May I ask who's calling?"

Offer to assist misdirected callers. You may be the only contact the caller has with the company and you can make an excellent first impression which tends to be remembered.

Don't chew gum, drink, eat anything or shuffle papers while talking to the caller. The sound goes right through the phone to their ear and leaves an unprofessional image.

Answer the phone as soon as it rings. It might be a million dollar order or the boss's wife...both equally important.

Speak directly into the telephone mouthpiece when talking for the clearest sound. Some people prop the handset under their chins with their head bent against it so their hands are free. The caller will then hear your muffled and distracted voice. Consider a headset if this is a problem.

Speak, or spell, names and numbers slowly and clearly so the caller has a chance to write them down without asking for a repeat.

Give the caller the option of holding or having a call returned. Don't be too quick to put people "on hold". Everyone hates to be "hanging on hold" even if there is music. If the caller wants to hold, an occasional "I haven't forgotten you" or "He's still busy" will be greatly appreciated.

Don't be intimidated by the telephone caller. Many answers are not at your fingertips in an instant. Admit when you don't have the answer, but offer to find out and call them back. If it takes longer than a day, call back and tell the individual you haven't forgotten them and you are still researching the issue or getting an answer for them.

Take time to instruct temporary personnel on the correct way to answer the phone, offer helpful telephone techniques and explain the general business of the department. Have them use an organization chart, if permitted, or internal telephone directory to get information and convey professionalism to the caller.

Inform temporary help not to respond with the dreaded "I'm only a temp" response. This portrays a negative connotation of a "don't know" or "don't care" attitude and could send the wrong signal to the caller. Remember, you never know who's calling until you answer first.

SMILE as you talk on the phone. Your mood carries over the line to the caller.

Offer recognition to the boss's frequent callers. "Hello, Mr. Jones. It's good to hear from you again." Everyone likes to be remembered.

If warranted, follow-up with the caller, or their secretary or AA, to see that he was properly connected to the right person or received the correct information. It's amazing how thankful people are to think you cared enough to make sure they were helped or the information was adequate.

> For example, follow up on an internal vice-president's request for information with his secretary if it originated through your organization. You will be remembered and possibly rewarded with a good word for this extra effort.

Always have paper or message pads and working writing instruments ready before answering the phone. Most offices use duplicate message pads for follow-up.

Always put the date and time on a caller's message. Even a few minutes can cost or make money in business and possibly save lives in the medical field.

Ask for the proper spelling of the caller's name, company and their return number even if the caller says your boss has it. "May I take you number again, Mr. Jones, just in case he doesn't have it with him when he returns your call?" Verify his reach number by repeating it. If this is an important client, either Rolodex it or put it into the electronic contact log or planner.

The art of SCREENING CALLS is to do it so well that the caller doesn't realize it's being done. For example:

NO NAME GIVEN BY CALLER - "I'm sorry, but he (the boss) is unavailable at the moment. Can someone else help you?" or "May I tell him who called?"

CALLER GIVES NAME, BOSS WILL TALK TO CALLER - "Oh yes, Mr. Jones, he is expecting your call. I will transfer you now."

BOSS DOESN'T WANT TO TALK TO CALLER, WANTS HIM REFERRED - "Yes, Mr. Jones, we were expecting your call, but he is unavailable at the moment. He asked that I refer you to Mr. Joe Brown, our customer service representative to help you. May I transfer you to Mr. Brown now?" Also indicate to caller what the referred person's phone number is.

- Some bosses will not return calls unless they know:
    a. the caller's name
    b. the company name
    c. the purpose of the call

Your response to the caller may be, "May I tell him what the call is in reference to?" The caller will usually answer with "a" and "b" and usually "c" (from above). If not, ask politely.

If the call sounds like an unsolicited sales call or crank call, take as much information as the caller will give and pass it along to the boss. He (the boss) then has the final decision on returning the call, or not. With experience, you will learn to screen and get rid of these unwanted calls yourself or refer them to someone else.

If the boss doesn't want to speak with the unsolicited caller, a "He's not interested at this time" will usually suffice.

Finally, what if your boss's boss calls and he is in his own staff meeting or unavailable? It varies from boss to boss, but cover yourself with your own boss's preference when higher ups are looking for him. One boss I worked for solved the problem with my responding "He's in a staff meeting with his team. Would you like me to interrupt?" That way, the choice is his.

Get in the habit of putting telephone messages in the same place each time and make sure your boss knows the spot.

Conference calls will be discussed in Chapter 8.

4
Schedules & Calendar Management

...Vying for precious time!

UNTIL YOU LEARN how to effectively manage yours and the boss's calendar, you may feel the only thing a calendar tells you is how many meetings or phone calls you've missed during the day. This section will help you make appointments for the boss, schedule appointments for others to see him, arrange travel and conferences and learn the value of keeping THREE calendars concurrently - two for him and one for you, i.e. see the PERPETUAL CALENDAR next page.

When booking time on the boss's calendar, be sure to get:

a. Dates
b. Times and duration of event
c. Topic (s) to be discussed
d. Attendees
e. Location (building, floor, room number, etc.)
f. Secretary's or AA's name and phone number handling it

g. Equipment requirements (A/V, whiteboard, markers, easel with paper)
h. Whether boss is just attending or responsible for presenting

Confirm appointments or meetings tentatively until approval with him.

When approving meetings with the boss, ask if he wants anyone else in his group to attend with him and does he require a pre-meeting briefing session.

You, as his secretary or AA, need to be in "calendar control" so you know what's going on. If he books calendar time on his own, chances are you will be the last to know. Don't be afraid to tell him "In order to keep you on schedule, I need to know what your schedule *is*. I'd be glad to update the calendar for you." This usually works!

THE PERPETUAL CALENDAR: This technique requires THREE identical calendars. One of them is switched daily with the boss at night with his next day 3"x5" schedule card inside (or electronic planner). This enables both you and he to have the latest update of his schedule at any given time. While updating his "old" calendar, this is a good time to check and see if he has made any schedule changes, notations or appointments for himself. *These calendars should be identical in every respect*, including telephone reference numbers.

To help you remember whether you changed calendars with him, you can label them "office" and "home" (on the inside cover) or spell his name on one and his initials on the other.

You, too, will keep an identical calendar at your desk for your own reference. The best times to update all calendars is at the end of the day and a recheck first thing in the morning.

He will soon get into the routine of switching calendars with you before he leaves the office.

Calendars are not set in concrete. The professional secretary or AA soon learns to juggle the boss's calendar to accommodate other attendees' schedules. Compromise and negotiation are helpful skills in calendar management.

It is necessary to learn the hierarchy of meeting importance for effective scheduling. In other words, whose meeting outranks whom? For example, your boss's meeting may be slipped to accommodate his boss's meeting. Most often, your boss's meetings are as important as his peer's meetings, but all take a back seat when it is *their* boss calling a meeting. Experience as well as his boss's secretary will help you understand priorities and politics within the company or corporation.

As soon as a meeting is scheduled, set up a file folder with the meeting title, date, time and location in order to have a place to put pertinent information from that time forward. Most meeting data is filed for future reference anyway, so you get a head start on organization. Also add a copy in your meeting binder (see next page).

You can often take more initiative booking internal meeting and appointments than you can with external ones. Always check with the boss first on outside requests so as not to compromise him or the company.

When a meeting is first booked, have the boss designate a "responsible for" person to assist him with meeting preparation and presentation, if required (could be the AA or yourself). Also schedule "run through" time on the calendar if role play or speech rehearsal time is needed (including VU graphs or digital PowerPoint presentations).

Take travel and transit time into consideration when booking meetings whether they be across the hall, across town or across the country or ocean. Have meeting location maps emailed or sent to out-of-town participants.

Always check meeting location preferences with the boss. Usually, subordinates will come to his office or a nearby meeting room and he will usually go to his superior's office for a meeting. However, he may want to appear "approachable" and visit subordinates' locations. You may even suggest and schedule time for these more casual "float abouts".

Don't forget to order refreshments or meals, depending on the meeting times, duration, budget and company policy.

For my own reference, I kept two binders of meeting notices. One is labeled "Present Month Meetings" and the second is labeled "Future Meetings". In the "Present Month..." binder, I have numbered dividers 1-31 for the days of that particular month. All other months are in the "Future..." binder where I filed by month, not individual days.

I can't count the number of times that bosses, at the last minute, can't locate their folder for an impending meeting (left it at home, etc.). At least with my meeting binder I can reproduce a copy of the meeting notice which will tell him: 1) where the meeting is to be held, 2) attendees, 3) duration, and 4) meeting objectives. The binder also serves as a reference for the secretary in case she needs to reach or track down her boss during the meeting.

The boss's meeting file folder should be tagged with a "Special Attention" or "Action" sticker to highlight its importance to him.

Use *all* of your boss's time efficiently! Most of my bosses were not adverse to having meetings take place during the lunch hour. I would order lunch for the meeting and then allow an extra half-hour in the meeting schedule so they could eat at a comfortable pace while they talked.

Another way to help bosses manage their time and efforts is to put as much information at their fingertips as possible without overburdening them. Bosses are always looking for telephone numbers. The following are suggested numbers to put in their pocket planners or notebooks, their cell phone or other electronic organizer, and their laptops or tablets:

- Office and home fax
- Family work and school
- Relatives' work or home numbers, as needed
- Key subordinates
- Your own home and cell numbers
- His superior's office and home
- Vacation home and other numbers, as appropriate.

Managing time and schedules for others is much like being a successful juggler. You have to keep several things in the air at the same time and be able to quickly adjust to changing situations. Like juggling, it takes time and practice on the secretary's part to assure a smooth performance for the boss.

Here's to a great meeting!

5
Files

...Not necessarily drudgery

THERE IS NO one "best" filing system that is applicable for all office situations. If this is one of your job functions, know that many companies and bosses usually have a filing system in place when you're hired. However, it may be possible to either change or suggest change if it is unwieldy and inefficient.

The main rule for a workable filing system is that YOU be able to retrieve the information when needed and that others in the office understand your system when you are absent.

Remember, the main uses of files are to: 1) store important and irreplaceable information for company and legal requirements, 2) be able to save and retrieve the same information quickly when your boss wants it and, 3) keep clutter both off the desks and out of your mind. This section deals with file management and "tickle" or "bring up" files.

One of the most important parts of the filing system is the "key" or "legend" which shows how the filing system works. This is necessary for all those using the files plus future temporary help. Color coding helps.

Another important part is knowing and understanding WHAT you are filing, WHAT it should be named and under what HEADING it should be filed. If in doubt, take the file to the boss, or his EA, and ask "If you wanted this particular file, what would you ask for?" or "What would you file this under?" By doing this, you are both on the same page and at the start of a successful filing system. Make your filing system work for you. It should be an asset to you and to the company, not a liability.

All companies have document retention guidelines for legal and tax purposes which must be strictly adhered to. You need to understand and enforce the retention policy since your boss may inadvertently toss something which needs to be retained. When in doubt, check with him or the company legal or tax experts. Also, there may be different retention guidelines for various job levels within the company, e.g. the President, Vice Presidents, Directors, Managers, etc.

As a general rule, files should be kept locked up when not in use. Most companies have policies for securing restricted or proprietary information, especially if your company does business with U.S. government contracts. It is essential that you abide by those rules to the letter. It is best to treat ALL files as if they were proprietary. This will protect both you and your boss and reduce the risk of industrial espionage.

Keys or combinations to locked files should be kept by you, your boss and I suggest, the secretary of your boss's boss. Therefore, some people may think twice about asking for a file if neither of you are there and perhaps that person should not have access to that file. Also, before giving copies of file papers to anyone not on the original distribution list, always check with your boss first and keep track of who gets that copy.

During your busy workday, there is much verbal and written "clutter" which constantly bombards the mind or inbox. This is usually information or data which doesn't require immediate action, but will at a later date. If it's verbal, write it down on a pad and date it. Otherwise, use the paper on which you received it. An efficient secretary or AA will use a "tickle" or "bring-up" file as an everyday routine in concert with her Schedules and Calendar Management as discussed in the last chapter.

My own tickle file system was a separate file folder or drawer with 1-31 dividers corresponding to each day of the current month. Behind that, I kept 12 dividers, one for each month in which to keep items that will come up in the future. I checked in the dated divider each morning before I worked on the calendars. The key to success with this system is to DO IT DAILY, no exceptions. Remind your temporary replacements to also do it daily.

I also used two "action binders". One was for items requiring my boss's response. The second binder was for other responses which were due TO my boss. Some items will fall into both binders, i.e. my boss needs to respond to a request. It would be filed in HIS action binder. When he refers that to someone to prepare a response for him, another copy goes into "responses due to" him. It is then easy to check status on items that are due and still outstanding. Always file the incoming request with the response for future reference.

Share your tickle file system with your boss and ask him to give you his "clutter" notes and reminders for inclusion in your file. It's very hard for any information, meetings, due dates or action items to slip by you if this successful method is used.

If not using electronic or computer software planners and file systems, Rolodex cards work just fine. I used colored cards for fast recognition - Pink for personal, Blue for business, Orange for references and Yellow for group members. Color is very helpful. Try in on the boss too.

Another hint is to make individual files for those with numerous pieces of paper floating around. For example, I made 26 individual hanging files for each letter of the alphabet and put individual file folders into these for each category that begins with that letter. Examples are below:

A - Overall alpha file category for hanging folder:
Apartment - file folder 1,
    Audio - file 2, Auto - file 3, etc.

B- Overall alpha file category for hanging folder:
Budget 2017 - file folder 1,
    Budget 2016 - file 2, Budget 2015 - file 3, Business Plan 2017 - file 4, etc.
    (Alphabet C through R)

S - Overall alpha file category for hanging folder:
Sales Budget 2017 - file folder 1, Sales Forecast 2017 - file 2, Sales Results 2016 - file 3, etc.

Use colored tabs to help break down your sections. For example, if you have a section called "Budget Files" in with all the other files, use a red tab for ALL budget files for immediate recognition when you open the drawer.

Many companies are using electronic or computer filing for general office routines. The key here is to BACKUP all files on other disks, hard drives, flash drives or in the Cloud on a regular basis to prevent total loss. I still liked to have a paper copy of the most important documents filed somewhere since computers seem to "crash" just before you need to retrieve a file.

I also found cross-filing extremely helpful. If you feel an item should logically be in two files simultaneously, by all means make a copy and put them there. The idea is to make an item easy to find, not keep the thinnest files. If you are torn whether to cross-file an item or not, chances are you *should* cross-file it.

I used to hate filing and stacked it in a pile for that "magical" day when I had nothing else to do. We all know that day never seems to come. Instead of thinking of filing as a hardship, turn it around and make it an important tool of your job. Keep it current and make it an asset. Save that "magical" day for cleaning out useless files and information.

Try to keep on top of filing as it accumulates quickly. An efficient file system makes everyone's work a lot easier... especially yours.

6
Crisis Management

...Murphy's Law & *YOU*!

SIMPLY PUT, MURPHY'S Law states that if something *can* go wrong, it *will* go wrong. How often is this true in the daily life of a businessman and his staff? Too often schedules go awry, people don't show up, meeting lunches are late, computers crash, presenters get sick, flights are delayed, files get misplaced or destroyed, coffee gets spilled on shirts and ties, people get panicky, blood pressures rise, palms get sweaty and cold, etc., etc. Sound familiar? Relax. There is hope and you can have fun solving problems in advance.

CONTINGENCY PLANNING PAYS OFF! Expect the unexpected and have a back-up plan for it. Most crises occur when there is a complete void of information, or direction, needed for resolution of a problem. The secret is to anticipate the problem and have already worked out a solution in advance. You don't have to belong to a "think tank" to make scenarios of potential office disasters. Just do "what if?" games in your head and outline a remedy. Then *write it down!* No, it won't solve every crisis, but it may handle most of them.

For example, the boss has a 10:00 am meeting scheduled in his office and he has to be across town by 11:00. Ask yourself "what if his 10:00 is late? What if he gets tied up on the phone? What if his car won't start or he gets lost on his way to his 11:00?" Again, the secret is to PLAN FOR THE UNEXPECTED. Why not call the 10:00 attendees at 9:30 and see if they will be punctual? Why not slip a next meeting reminder note to the boss? Why not give him a highlighted route map to his 11:00?

These questions and possible solutions may sound simple and sometimes silly, but they happen every day in offices in some form or another. It's kind of fun to creatively devise "what if" scenarios and solutions. I'm not trying to make you paranoid, but try it a few times and you, as well as your boss, will be pleased with your advance planning and solutions to potential problems.

The following are some helpful hints to fill that information void we discussed earlier:

Always have reach numbers for everyone...office and home.

Take a few extra minutes at the end of each day to get ready for tomorrow and anticipate any problems. You will be glad you did the next morning.

Have reach numbers of office building managers or "supers" as well as building security or alarm services.

Have reach numbers of conference or meeting rooms and the number of a secretary or AA nearest to it.

Copy or duplicate computer files for backup OFTEN during the day in case of power failure, brownouts, or when you're away from your desk. This prevents panic when you have worked so hard on a long letter or a project. There are software "utilities" available that do this easily for you. Contact your IT person, if applicable.

Have emergency or weekend numbers for your boss's superiors and subordinates, travel agencies, travel coordinators, limo services and carriers like UPS, FedEx or DHL. Keep this list at the office and *at home*.

Arrange to have a single line telephone set programmed as a "power failure station" (if PBX) near a window in case of switchboard and/or power failure. This allows the boss or you to call outside and see how to dial with the available light from the window. Cell phones have greatly eliminated the need for this.

Have more than one set of desk or file keys for the boss and yourself kept with strategic people in the company like his EA or maybe another secretary so files can be accessed if you are out.

Have extra computer supplies, batteries for clocks and calculators and other non-rechargeable electronics, projector bulbs, pens and refills, extra VU graph supplies, an extension cord and extra long USB cables well in advance of the need.

Use a spiral binder or steno pad to keep track of "Things To Do" and cross them off as completed. Save the paper for future reference (for a reasonable time).

Allow "run over" time for meetings and phone calls.

If your boss's and/or his subordinates are out of the office, make sure you know who has his "delegation of authority" to act on matters that may arise.

Reconfirm, in advance, any services that are expected on a certain date and time like airline flights, luncheon deliveries, sub-contracted orders, limo reservations, etc.

Have club soda or stain remover available for coffee and tea stains in clothing.

When things "get out of hand", take a walk or step away from your desk for a few minutes to compose yourself.

Contingency planning DOES pay off! Take time to play the "what if" game both with yourself and the boss and come up with acceptable alternatives to defeat old Mr. Murphy.

7
Is it Lunchtime Already?

...From popcorn to paté

LUNCH IS NOT an insignificant event in today's business, social and professional world. It is considered extended work time in many companies. Deals are made or broken over lunches and there are many books and articles on "power" luncheons. This section is not intended to discuss the psychology of luncheon behavior, but rather to deal with the mechanics of a successful one.

There are basically two types of lunches - one where the boss eats OUT, usually with customers and one when he eats IN, usually a working lunch in the office with staff or peers. We will look at "eating in" more closely.

HINTS FOR EATING **OUT**:
Find out what restaurants the boss likes. Visit them and get to know the manager and staff. Get menus for advance ordering during rushed meetings. Sample the food and service and let the boss know what you think. Check to see if they cater. Get a receipt if the boss will reimburse you for your exploratory lunches.

Can the restaurant provide amenities such as birthday or celebration cakes for special clients? Order flowers? Provide a private dining room for large parties? Provide a favorite beverage? Comply with dietary or religious needs? Accommodate customers on short notice? Direct bill the company? Give corporate discounts? Most good restaurants will do these things gladly, some will not. It's better to find out in advance in order to avoid embarrassment later.

HINTS FOR EATING *IN*: THE WORKING LUNCH
When starting a job, find out the boss's preference for his own lunch or working meeting lunches. Write them down for reference and alternate his menus, as needed.

Don't feel it's "beneath you" to help serve lunch or offer coffee or sodas. In today's workplace, it shows a willingness to work as a team.

For a morning meeting, order coffee (regular & decaf), creamer, tea bags & hot water, bottled water, sugar and sugar substitutes. A suggested menu might be split bagels, mini-Danish with butter, cream cheese and jelly/jams on the side. Remember fruit and fruit juices.

With today's emphasis on fitness and health, order some salads for lunch such as tuna, egg, fruit or pasta. Also fresh fruits such as apples, bananas and seedless grapes.

Many are turning away from roast beef, salami and other high fat fare to chicken, turkey and tuna. Order a tray of lettuce, tomatoes, onions, pickles and olives for sandwiches with whole grain breads. Don't forget condiments like mayo, mustard, etc.

In addition to chips and pretzels, desserts such as cookies, cupcakes and candy are welcomed. Don't forget some low calorie options, as well.

For a PM break, have refills of coffee and hot water for teabags. Sodas (regular & diet), water and iced tea make good beverage choices for lunch. Bottled water will be appreciated too, including a few bottles of "designer" water such as Perrier, Evian in both carbonated (gas) and plain (no gas) varieties.

Order items to be delivered about 1/2 hour before the luncheon meeting begins so if there is a mix-up, you have time to rectify it. Also check condiments, napkins, silverware or plastic ware and cups or glasses in a sufficient quantity.

If the meeting has already started, have lunch set up in a nearby conference room or outside the meeting room so it may be delivered and prepared without interrupting the meeting itself. Then, to announce lunch, slip the boss a note saying "Lunch is ready when you are". They can return to the meeting room to eat if it is a working lunch.

After lunch, put leftover soda, potato chips, cookies or fruit in the conference room so they may be nibbled throughout the afternoon. Ice and cups may also be desired.

Confirm all food orders with the caterer, food service or company cafeteria *a day in advance* and actually check the order for correctness when it arrives. Keep a list of the order on your desk in case you are called away and someone else needs to confirm it. Write down such information as delivery time, who delivered it and what was ordered on your calendar in order to give feedback (good or bad) to the food supplier.

If your boss has the same frequent visitors for lunch, try to remember their favorite food, beverage or snack for the next time. You can put these preferences on the back of their Rolodex card, in your electronic contact database, in an address book or on the meeting calendar. Little amenities are greatly appreciated. One executive always stopped by my desk to say hello when he was near our office because I remembered to get him pretzels with his lunch, and I kept a bag of them in my desk drawer for him.

Successful working lunches are not a difficult task if you remember to treat the attendees, and your boss, the same way *you* would like to be treated at a luncheon. Take time for the special amenities; they are so important to all.

Bon Appétit!

8
Minutes, Meetings & Ice Cream

...Again, *planning*

SUCCESSFUL MEETINGS DON'T just happen. Care in preparation, covering all the bases and being ready for the unexpected, as we discussed earlier, all contribute to enjoyable and mutually beneficial meetings. As with crisis management, here are a few helpful suggestions for your next meeting:

Supply the receptionist with a list of attendees in case a call comes in. Ask the boss if he wants the meeting interrupted for anything other than an urgent call. If he doesn't, then you can distribute any messages during the break. If posting messages to a bulletin board, fold the message slip up to the person's name the call is for, thereby concealing the name of the caller and the message.

Pre-designate telephones to be used for returning calls unless they use their cell phones. Don't allow the attendees to use nearby desks for returning calls since the desk's tenant may return and any proprietary material on a person's desk may be compromised.

Announce the meeting will restart in five minutes for any stragglers in the hallway or any group conversations going on outside the meeting room.

Have pads, pencils, ballpoint pens, easels with paper or whiteboards with colored and erasable markers plus an eraser. Also thumbtacks, tape and VU graph supplies should be kept handy, if needed. For yourself, if attending the meeting, have pens of different colors to mark important points for recap or transcription later in your minutes.

If there is a published agenda for the meeting, have extra copies on the conference room table for newcomers or attendees who forgot to bring theirs.

Some bosses prefer to distribute agendas with just "AM" and "PM" designated instead of a strict timetable showing the actual duration of time each person or particular topic has. A drawback to this is that someone, perhaps you, has to monitor and enforce the time so all agenda topics can be covered.

Supply the boss with a list of attendees so that he, or you, can check them off as they arrive and know if he needs to wait for anyone else before starting the meeting. If teleconferencing is being used too, after setting it up orally or by email, reconfirm the day before with all participants. Have the callers "on-line" prior to the boss arriving.

If you sit in on a meeting, select a seat just inside the door so that anyone opening the door can give you messages instead of walking in and disrupting the meeting. It also gives you the advantage to "slip out" unobtrusively, if necessary.

Familiarize yourself with the conference equipment such as computers and digital projectors, VU graph machines, slide projectors, telephones and microphones so you can help presenters prepare. They may be nervous when speaking in front of an audience and forget how the equipment works. These are a few minutes well spent when *you* are called on and asked *how* it works.

MEETING MINUTES SHOULD CONTAIN: 1. Date and time of meeting, 2. Name of meeting, 3. Subject of meeting, 4. Names of invited attendees and companies, if from outside, including names of alternate representatives for those unable to attend, 5. Copies of previous minutes for reference and follow-up. Distribute as needed if agreed to by the boss, 6. Crucial points said and *who* said them, 7. Rebuttals or reactions by *whom*, 8. Action items and *who* is responsible for each, and 9. Approximate date of next meeting

It is difficult to initially decide what to write down unless you understand the purpose of the meeting and the desired outcomes. Many bosses will already have this in the form of an outline on paper or write it on an easel or whiteboard. It is always a good idea to copy whatever is written since it may help to reconstruct an idea later, or take a picture of it with a cell phone.

You may need help from someone attending the meeting who understands the important points and will indicate to you "Take this down" or, after discussion, the boss may say "Write down these action items". Remember to take all easel papers with you and erase whiteboards or blackboards after the meeting.

The natural fear most secretaries feel when asked to "take minutes" of a meeting can be greatly overcome by getting to know what your boss, or the meeting chairman, is trying to accomplish in the meeting. The best way to know the purpose is simply ask beforehand what he wishes to have happen in the meeting and what points you should listen for and write down.

After some experience, many bosses and their secretaries have a "secret" communication signal to denote important aspects that need to be recorded - a nod of the head, a wave of the hand or direct verbal communication to record a certain item.

Don't be afraid to say "Slow down, please" if the meeting is going too fast, getting out of hand or causing you to get behind in your note taking. After all, your boss and the attendees are counting on *you* for an accurate account of the meeting points.

I have worked meetings with another secretary who also recorded the information so that if I missed something, she would have a backup for comparison. Most secretaries don't have this luxury so you must remain alert. Use of a digital tape recorder or smart phone recording makes your job easier, but some meeting attendees may object to being recorded. Don't use one unless you have full agreement from the boss and/or the participants.

Probably the hardest part of taking minutes is to decide what really should be written down and distributed to the attendees, especially when everyone seems to be talking at once. After a heated meeting, I may ask the chairman to summarize the outcome of the discussion after the meeting and any action items that should appear in the minutes. A properly run meeting should have a summary at the end of resolutions, action items, due dates, and individual or group responsibilities.

If VU graphs or PowerPoint slides are used by a presenter, ask for a paper copy or have the file emailed to you. Always obtain permission from the presenter to reproduce and use any of their material in the published minutes.

It is important to write up your notes as soon as possible after the meeting in order to retain the freshness of both your thoughts and your handwritten notes. It's amazing how hard it is sometimes to decipher your own writing when you look at it later. Present a draft copy of the notes to the boss for his editorial proofing before the minutes are distributed. Remember to mark the copies "Proprietary" or "Restricted", if applicable.

When distributing copies of the minutes, check with your boss to see if he wants copies sent to ALL invitees or just those in attendance, or perhaps both. A copy should also be put in the meeting folder for filing. If you know when the next meeting is scheduled, make a label and file and put in a copy of the minutes you just did. This will save you from hunting for last month's meeting minutes when someone asks what happened at the last meeting.

For a memorable mid-afternoon snack, in addition to the standard sodas, coffee and tea, order a variety of ice creams (bars, cups, sandwiches) in different flavors. *Everyone loves ice cream!* Get extra napkins, a bowl of fruit and extra bottled water for that ice cream thirst.

There are many good books and magazine articles on meeting etiquette, rules of order and minutes preparation. Take time to study these resources if meetings are a major part of your job responsibilities.

Also, the better you know your company and its products, or your profession and your boss's responsibilities within it, the more confident you will become in meeting sessions and/or taking down the minutes.

9
Birthdays, Balloons & Thank Yous

...*YOU* are his memory!

YOU, AS THE boss's secretary, become a member of his "extended family" in a manner of speaking. Very often, he spends more time with you at work than with his own family at home. He needs for *you* to be his memory, not only for office matters, but for many of the personal remembrances he may often overlook or forget.

This aspect of the job may not have a high priority in most secretaries' view, but it may very well be of the utmost importance to his functioning in both his business and personal life. There are easy ways to accomplish this task of remembering for him.

On both his calendars and yours, list all important family occasions in RED (birthdays, anniversaries, kid's sporting events, recitals, etc.). SEE TICKLE FILE in Chapter 5. When first starting these calendar reminders, you should ask him for the dates and then initiate a call to his wife (with his permission, of course) to double-check events, dates and to solicit her input for other important items. Thereafter, a monthly or quarterly check with her will keep both calendars up to date.

Remind him not only of birthdays, anniversaries and other pleasant things, but also of illnesses, deaths, friends or acquaintances in hospitals, nursing homes, etc.

Also acknowledge accomplishments of business acquaintances, employee service anniversaries, peers, friends and college chums as well as neighborhood accomplishments (school board election, promotions, newspaper articles about them, etc.).

A personal letter from the boss to employees thanking them for contributions to company objectives, company charities, United Way participations and other civic activities is always appreciated. *You* may be asked to write these letters for his review and signature.

When the boss and his wife are booked for an occasion (through work), you should inform them of the appropriate dress (black tie, informal, casual, etc.). This should include notification of both business and personal functions. The spouse may ask you if other spouses are attending in case they want to confer on dress or activities.

His birthday is very important even though he may not make a fuss over it. All bosses like recognition too and a "Happy Birthday" balloon or two along with cake and ice cream plus a card signed by "the gang" bring out the kid in every executive. Even getting a "It's my Birthday" pin for his lapel will make him feel doubly special on *his* day. *Note: Others may not wish to acknowledge their birthday. Be sure you know their preference.*

Be sure to include your *own* birthday on his calendar in RED, of course, since you're part of his "extended family".

Remind your boss when HIS boss has a birthday or other special occasion coming up. These dates can be obtained through your "secretarial network" within the company. More on this later.

For important events like service anniversaries, promotions, retirements or weddings, you should ask the boss if he would like to do something special like having a luncheon or purchasing a special gift for the person. Many companies have award catalogues to choose from.

Service anniversaries, new college graduates or additional degrees earned are usually obtained from your personnel department. If not, suggest whoever is in charge of human resources (HR) to start a file by day of the year so managers can commemorate special events.

Have some sympathy, get-well and congratulations cards in advance and stash them in your drawer or file cabinet. Don't wait until the occasion arises to buy them. By having them on hand, you make the boss appear empathetically responsive and the recipients will long remember his prompt thoughtfulness. Also have a variety of cards with various levels of expression so he can select the one he deems appropriate.

Buy a sheet of stamps for his use and keep them in *your* desk so you will know when you are running low.

I do not mean to imply that you should fund the above items. Anticipate expenses and ask the boss in advance for enough money for the "kitty" to cover stamps, sodas, snacks, greeting cards, etc. Too often, many secretaries do not ask for the money and wind up paying for it themselves while harboring an ill feeling for his "Scroogeness". Remember, he or the company can afford it better than you can.

There may be an expense account or voucher system which can be used for these purposes. Check company policy or the boss's preference to determine whether these are allowable expenses for company reimbursement. It may also vary by management level.

Type reminders on his daily 3"x5" schedule card or electronic device that may include events he desires to remember both on and off the job. For example, Bill's birthday at work or his neighbor Sam's anniversary. If the event occurs on a weekend or when he's out of town, put it on his Friday card or one nearest to the date *before* he leaves.

DON'T LET ANYONE FORGET SECRETARY'S OR ADMIN ASSISTANT'S DAY!
A short, thoughtful, even humorous note to all bosses or their EAs in the organization approximately two weeks before the date will help jog memories for their own staff. If other secretaries report to you or to him, you might remind him in person and asks what he thinks is appropriate for the occasion. Put it in *his* calendar too.

A thank you note to other secretaries in the organization on Secretary's Day from you would be much appreciated. Very often their support is necessary all year long to make you look good to your boss.

It will also be appreciated if you remember other secretaries with a card or little inexpensive gifts on their birthdays, holidays and other special occasions. Your thoughtfulness will pay off handsomely when you need their support in crisis situations.

DON'T FORGET THE BOSS ON BOSS'S DAY! A card, a homemade goodie or even a verbal reminder will be appreciated by him and other bosses in the company.

Company and personal Christmas cards and/or holiday business gifts may become your responsibility. With proper time and planning, the holiday need not be difficult or time consuming. A good time to remind the boss is around October 1st, especially if cards need to be ordered and/or personalized. Give yourself time for you or him to sign them personally. Don't forget friends and business associates of different faiths or religious preferences during the Christian holidays. Remember that Chanukah falls on an earlier date each year. A special card for these occasions will be especially meaningful. Also, don't use Christmas seals or religious stamps on these envelopes.

If ordering cards, you can show the boss the catalog, brochures or samples for him to select the ones he likes (or will probably leave it up to you). Don't leave the information in his in-box as you may not get his response in time.

If recipients are overseas, allow extra time for international and APO mailings. The Post Office usually recommends mailing by early December to ensure arrival by Christmas (Air Mail). Different countries may require different postage amounts for the same card. Get receipts for reimbursement.

It is a good idea to insert business cards in customer holiday mailings. Check to see you have sufficient cards on hand or if you need to order more.

Each company, corporation or profession has its own policy on giving and receiving of holiday gifts as well as their monetary value (the IRS does!). Get a clarification on these policies from, or for, the boss.

You may be given the responsibility of choosing holiday gifts for your boss. Don't despair. There are many "Personal Shopper" services at the better department stores as well as reputable mail order and online stores offering selections from food to books. They will wrap and ship in time for any occasion. Many will even personalize the gifts with the company logo or include your own holiday or business cards. Make it easy on yourself during those hectic times during the year.

Giving gifts to international customers or friends will involve more thought than with the office crowd. There are many social customs and gift restriction taboos the boss should be aware of when selecting a gift. The best approach is to first check with your staff, agent or sales rep overseas. Also check with online or local library etiquette publications. A mistake here could ruin a budding business relationship. Your Public Relations office, if applicable, might be able to help.

You will need a supply of "Thank You" notes for the boss's use in responding to gifts received during the holidays or other occasions. He may prefer to jot a note on personal stationery or on a personalized notepad. You will make it easier if you draft a reply for him reminding him of the gift, the giver and the occasion.

You might keep a "Personal Business" file for him, separate from the regular office business files, in which you file notations of cards or gifts (and the value) given or received. Then give the file to him at the end of the year for his personal or business tax records. Again, check with your boss for his preference on handling gifts.

Since *you* are his memory, be sure not to forget his *personal* special days; i.e. his wife's birthday, Mother's Day, etc. I always ask a week before the date "Would you like to send roses to your wife for her birthday next week?" I certainly don't mind doing this for him, but I hate a last minute request as he flies out the door "Order some flowers and have them delivered *today*!" Be kind to yourself and plan ahead. Oh, by the way, be sure to remind him when he leaves the office that *he* ordered pink roses for his wife's birthday and they will be delivered tomorrow. Also remind him of what he sent her last time.

Of all the aspects of a secretary's or admin assistant's job, *remembering* and *reminding* your boss is one of the most important and rewarding parts of your job. Surveys of executives confirm how really dependent they are on your ability to organize their time and their lives.

There are many electronic organizers, smart phones and other memory devices on the market today and many bosses either have or will buy one. Be sure to buy two so you will have an identical one as the boss. The major problem with these is that someone has to input and update the information within them and this job may fall on you.

Don't be intimidated by these gadgets, but simply inject your personal "touch" as you would with his typed schedule cards or itinerary.

10
Getting & Building Support

...Up, down & across

A PHRASE I'M reminded of when thinking about building and maintaining a support infrastructure is "No man is an island unto himself". This is especially true in today's modern business and professional world where overused buzzwords like "networking", "linkage", "strategize" and "24/7" are today's mantras.

Even rarer today to find is the modern, professional and successful secretary or administrative assistant who is a loner. True, there are many old films which portray either the crabby, snooty, spinster secretary of the only banker in town or the young, dumb pretty thing who sits doing nothing except chewing gum and filing her nails. These stereotypes are way outdated as we gain a foothold in the 21st century.

The modern assistant must be a collector, mover and manager of large amounts of information in order to efficiently assist the boss in his daily routine. This information movement must be done with good judgment, speed and discretion in order to meet the demands and deadlines of the job.

Building a strong support infrastructure within your company or organization is not, I repeat *not*, an overnight process. True, you may feel a false sense of power as the boss's secretary and expect quick answers and people to jump when you speak. Come on down from your ivory tower and realize that others are responding to the position and power of the boss and not you. Support is built from trust, loyalty, helpfulness, understanding and friendliness, NOT from aloofness, threat or coercion.

Learning to use the resources available to you is a good place to start. If you are new on the job, someone is usually assigned to "show you the ropes". This is your first link in your network. Other introductions will follow and soon you will get to know several people within a small, close-knit organization. In many businesses or professions, people tend to "herd" into small groups or cliques depending on their job function, education, social status or personality. Some secretaries also like to gather within the confines of the secretarial "pool" or behind the doors or plush carpet of executive row.

This syndrome is not enough in today's demand for job excellence. Your circle of knowledge and influence must be widened to include almost every facet of the business or profession and to key in on those individuals who can help you understand their roles and responsibilities. Curiosity can be a great asset here. Get to know people, what they do and how they do it. It's very interesting!

By understanding their roles, you are starting to build your network for later use in obtaining information and help, when needed. Maintaining these relationships takes time, friendliness, reciprocity, and genuine interest in the people themselves. A good beginning building block is based on mutual helpfulness. Many around you also need information in order to do their own jobs more effectively and efficiently. An offer to help them opens the door to building strong, beneficial relationships.

I enjoyed being that person who offered to indoctrinate secretarial staff into the business. It not only gives the opportunity to train someone correctly, but allowed a certain "bonding" to occur between the newcomer and myself which can last throughout your working career. As an "advisor" though, you have a great responsibility not only to the new person, but also to the company to transfer positive, constructive training and advice.

If we could eliminate the negative phrase "that's not my job" from our everyday working vocabulary, then both we and the company would benefit from the increased morale and productivity found when everyone strives to satisfy the customer or client. I certainly don't mean to imply you should do other people's jobs, but instead help instill in both new and old coworkers that everyone has a stake in the "job" of customer or client satisfaction. It really *is* everyone's job!

Remember, too, each of us is a customer or client to someone else within our own company or organization in addition to those outside our business walls. Passing these values along to others will help build the quality of your network as they will come to see and respect your values toward quality output in your daily interactions.

Many people overuse the networking concept and are viewed as selfish or greedy "climbers" to their peers. One should temper good judgment with discretion when building an information foundation.

Learn to network wherever you are: while taking a training course, at lunch, social functions, retirement or birthday parties, etc. Don't just network with other secretaries alone. Branch out! Be curious and ask people what they do and how they do it. Everyone loves to talk about themselves, their jobs and their achievements. File this information away for later use when the boss or your coworkers have an information need.

Networking doesn't happen just at work. It is part of the day-to-day living experience in a changing, complex world both at work and home.

11
Are Desktop Computers Obsolete?

...Technology tools are changing!

LET'S FACE IT, the days of manual and electric typewriters, mimeographs, Dictaphone machines, thermal fax machines and perhaps even desktop computers have almost become extinct in American commerce. Although computers, in general, are here to stay, the newest buzzwords and technologies are smart phones, Apple, Android, the Cloud and all-in-one smart printers with copier, scanner, fax and wireless technology capabilities built-in.

Yes, it is necessary to learn how to use the newest gadgets, but don't worry, you can have job security. There will always be a need for those who also know *how to use* the latest tools.

The computing power alone in these small, hand-held smart phones contain far more memory, features and processing capabilities than the computers on the Apollo missions to land men on the moon. It's not science fiction anymore!

As long as there are human bosses and managers, there will be a need for a human interface to the business and that person is *you*. Computers are still only as good as their input and somewhat ease workload, but don't eliminate a lot of paper as was hoped in the beginning of the computer age. Artificial intelligence is just beginning to appear, but will never replace, I believe, the personal and professional duty of a good secretary or administrative assistant.

Technologies change daily and companies will buy new computers, gadgets and programs which you will have to learn to keep ahead of your job. Yes, you will need to improve your skills on applications such as word processing, graphics, spreadsheets and presentation programs as new software releases come out.

A lot of bosses may not learn to utilize computing skills effectively, but they will expect *you* to master them. A good working knowledge of the Microsoft Office suite of software, for example, gives you a solid foundation for secretarial or administrative assistant roles in your organization just like accounting software is essential in a financial organization.

The purpose of this section is NOT to teach computer skills or software programs, but rather be aware of how helpful programs can be to your organization's efficiency and productivity. If you have an Information Technology (IT) department, they can provide training and assistance with equipment and software programs and problems. Computers will crash and you will lose pages of correspondence unless you BACKUP your work frequently. I cannot emphasize this enough!

A key element of a successful office computer operation is STANDARDIZATION of software systems. It is much more efficient to have everyone using the *same* word processing, database, graphics or spreadsheet system, especially when secretaries cover each other's jobs and are familiar with the same software on any computer in the office. Training costs, too, are reduced, but the main advantages of standardization are the increased productivity and efficiency in the office information handling operations.

Sometimes you may have input to the computer and software buying decision process. If possible, have your boss use the services of an unbiased computer systems consultant who can study your business needs and then recommend the best hardware and software solutions to meet your company's information processing objectives.

The long-term cost of a properly designed system will be much lower than one piece-parted together in which you will often outgrow both in features and functionality in the near-term. Although computing costs are still dropping, the expense of changing out systems and retraining personnel frequently is hard to justify in either dollars or efficiency. Look for scalable systems to meet your needs as your company grows.

If you are a lone secretary or in a small secretarial group within a smaller office environment, then you may be selected to choose an appropriate software system for the office. There are many excellent programs on the market today. Look for one that:

- is *popular* and a *best seller* for your purpose
- is *updated frequently* as new features are added
- provides *"toll-free"* telephone operating & technical assistance
- has an *online help menu* and *online operating manual*

- offers *training programs online* and through dealer networks
- gets *good user reviews* and is *easy to use*.

It's definitely a technology-changing world and many secretaries now say they "...can't believe how I ever got along without my laptop or smart phone". The same thing was said when I started out after high school about the electric typewriter, carbon paper, the mimeograph and Dictaphone machine when these were new. Good luck with the change... and stay ahead of it!

12
Communicating with Your Boss

...Sometimes *not* so easy

THE MOST IMPORTANT part of communicating with your boss is the ability to talk freely and openly concerning both business and personal issues plus the ability to resolve real or potential conflicts between yourselves. This is often harder to do than it sounds and may take a lot of practice and patience on your part to be a good communicator.

SET UP THE GROUND RULES - If you are new on the job, schedule time to sit down with the new boss and really try to understand what the job function is and what he expects of you. Just ask him! Find out what and who is important to him and what his likes and dislikes are. If there is a job description, ask if it has changed any and, if there isn't one, offer to write one for his approval. The boss may also ask his Executive Assistant (EA) to cover this with you.

Discuss the regular working hours and the overtime or compensation (comp) time off for extra work hours. Make him aware of any special circumstances you may have such as evening classes or the need to pick up children by a certain time which may conflict with the working hours. Most of the time these issues are subject to negotiation and compromise. A good start toward effective communication is mutual understanding of the basic job requirements and of you and your boss's expectations.

It is a little more difficult if you have been on the job awhile and still feel there is a communication barrier between you and the boss. If the barrier centers around a particular event, you must "clear the air" and move on from there.

Every boss has a different personality and management style (Thank Goodness!) and there could be conflict with your personalities or your acceptance of his style. This is probably the worst case scenario and you'll have to "bite the bullet" and openly discuss the issues. If you don't, then chances are you will continue to be unhappy, your performance will suffer and you could possibly be replaced or quit.

If no agreement or reconciliation is possible, then you must decide what is best for you and outline your options. Fortunately, most bosses welcome the chance to close the communication gap, but there are still those "...who can't keep a secretary".

GET IT OUT IN THE OPEN - How often have you read or been told that you shouldn't keep feelings hidden inside? Again, it is easier said than done, but it is essential to exchange thoughts in order to communicate effectively.

Don't run into his office and unload everything on him. Start small and get clarification on a single item that may be bothering you such as his use of obscenity or off-color jokes.

Try to be understanding and not defensive and try to see the problem from his point of view. You may or may not get resolution, but he becomes aware of the fact there is an issue bothering you and you are willing, and feel comfortable enough, to discuss it with him.

If you are shy, timid or defensive about opening the communication channel, there are other avenues of help available. Training courses on communication skills, assertiveness, negotiation principles and stress management are frequently offered within a company by an outside training company, community college adult education or online courses. Any training in the art of communications will be helpful to your career and advancement.

DEVELOP A CONFIDANT - Someone who is close to the boss can provide friendly and constructive feedback on problems or areas of conflict. Many bosses also prefer to use a third-party as a feedback mechanism rather than direct confrontation. Your confidant may turn out to be his Executive Assistant or another, or former, secretary. Listen, but don't judge the boss.

ADMIT WHEN YOU'RE WRONG - If you make a mistake, admit it, correct it and move on. Don't try a cover-up and pass the blame onto someone else if it was really your fault. We all know someone who blames others, but never themselves. It's a hard reputation to live down, especially at work. When you have erred, inform the boss ASAP so he is "covered" and can support your efforts or help to fix the problem. Mistakes can be viewed as part of a learning curve, risk-taking in the job, lack of training or experience or just poor judgment. It is essential to avoid these mistakes *twice*.

APPRAISALS AND PAY RAISES - Most companies and organizations have a well-defined appraisal and compensation plan. Smaller businesses and offices may not. You should certainly ask what the plan provisions are when you start a new job or change jobs and know the latitude within your own job category.

Learn how the appraisal process works and prepare yourself all year long by keeping commendation letters, recognition awards and training course completions in a separate personal file. Also keep track of special projects you participated in as well as unpaid overtime. It's easy to forget how many "extras" you did during the year when the annual appraisal time comes around. All these "attaboys" (or "attagirls") should be factored into your own appraisal input.

In the first chapter, one of the bosses interviewed said that "…a good secretary shouldn't have to ask for raises". Many times this is true, but there are exceptions. Most times, your boss is the first step in the appraisal and salary recommendation process and it doesn't hurt to remind him of your contributions during the year.

Some bosses need a gentle reminder when it is time for your job performance and salary review. Schedule a non-busy time with him when both your minds are not burdened with urgent things to do. Early mid-week mornings worked best for me as I caught his attention before others did.

If your boss is the type who tends to forget when salary reviews are due, then you should be well-prepared to document and present your achievements during the year. Your knowledge of the company's financial status will also be important for you to know. If the business has done well, then your arguments for a salary increase will be much stronger than if the company or business is not doing so well. In either case, focus on your performance, strengths and contributions.

If you do get the "it's been a bad year" speech, then it may be wise to remain silent afterwards and let your silence be your best spokesman. Many people feel uncomfortable when confronted with silence and this alone may work in your favor to receive the raise you deserve. Again, recap your accomplishments and let your past performance be your strongest asset. In Chapter 15 we discuss promotions in more detail.

CAREER PLANNING - This is also covered in Chapter 15, but by all means, make your boss aware of your career aspirations within the organization and company. Many want a career as a professional secretary or an Administrative Assistant while others may use the position as a stepping stone to staff or other management goals. Most managers and bosses recognize the qualities and performance found in good assistants are excellent credentials and predictors for future success in other areas of the business. They may want to create an opportunity for you by recommending you for other positions within the company.

Unfortunately, sometimes the secretarial pay does not keep pace with your responsibilities and one has to choose whether to be happy at the present salary or unhappy with another job at a little higher pay. The secretarial or AA's "ladder" for promotion is usually limited to the management "pyramid" structure and sometimes there are limited progression slots available. Sometimes, one has to choose to leave a smaller office or company and go with a larger corporation to achieve vertical growth in their career.

SAD, BUT TRUE - Another aspect of communications with the boss is establishing boundaries for respect, behavior and moral responsibility. At the first sign of inappropriate actions or behavior (sexual harassment, obscenity, etc.), discussion is vital to maintain a working and personal relationship. If nothing changes or cannot be worked out, a talk with Human

Resources may be necessary. If this doesn't provide relief, a transfer or even leaving the company may be necessary. This is a really tough one, but needs resolved immediately for a genial close working relationship. Document everything!

Again, openly communicate with your boss. It works!

13
When He's Ready to go Home

...Avoiding late night calls!

MANY BOSSES PREFER to have you pack their briefcase with homework and mail so they can just walk out the office at the end of the day (whatever time that may be). If this is your case, a suggested way is to "layer" his briefcase with the contents in order of importance *from the top down*:

- CALENDAR with schedule card attached for the next day
- MEETING folders for tomorrow in order of occurrence
- SIGNATURE folder with papers to be signed
- ACTION ITEMS folder with:

The "hottest" top priority piece with a "Special Attention" sticker can be attached to the outside with a rubber band around the entire folder in case this is the only material he gets to work on that night

Other pieces layered inside the action folder with the most important pieces on top and others in order of importance.

Importance can be determined by the originator (his boss & higher), due dates, etc.

GENERAL CORRESPONDENCE folder containing general business letters or memos requiring a normal response time.

READING folder for non-critical informational material. If he can't get to it for a couple of weeks, no problem.

DAILY NEWSPAPER(S) OR MAGAZINE(S) you know he likes to read.

OTHER HINTS AND SUGGESTIONS:
Check the briefcase to make sure there are sufficient business cards, favorite writing instrument (sharpened pencils, ink pen, ball-point pen with refills, etc.) and "buck slips", Post-It notes and routing slips for his responses. Check and refill paper clips, "Special Attention" and "Private" stickers as well as the writing tablet he prefers. Include a folder with several pieces of letterhead stationery and envelopes in case he needs to pen a quick letter away from the office.

Before he heads out, check and see if there is anything special he needs you working on first thing tomorrow morning in case he goes to a meeting first, is late coming in or is traveling away from the office.

Always notify him if *you* leave the office before he does in case there is something special he needs. An example might be if he's in a meeting and expecting an important phone call. It may sound trivial to you to inform him of your leaving, but he is often unaware of time. I would normally stay until his call came through.

Occasionally ask if he needs home office supplies such as writing tablets, staples, rubber bands, stickers, pens, etc.

If he uses a digital or micro-cassette recorder at home, furnish him with extra cassettes, labels, batteries or extra recharger. Also include an extra copy of the instruction manual to be left at home. It may come in handy.

For both company or personal cars, remind him of any servicing appointments and offer to make alternate transportation arrangements. If he takes it to the dealer himself, remind him of *who* and *where* on his schedule card, and arrangements of who will bring him to work.

If he has accepted a last minute invitation (dinner or drinks), remind him to call home before he leaves or offer to do this for him.

Most late night phone calls to you are a result of:

- Changing travel arrangements
- Thinking of something you need to do in the a.m. in case he's late
- He can't locate something or some information
- He calls you while on a trip
- He wants you to come in the office early
- He's mad about something
- His car is broken and needs a ride or other transportation in the a.m.

Some of these can be avoided through proper planning on your part, but not always. When he's traveling, *always* keep his itinerary and travel emergency numbers (airline, limo, airline club & frequent flyer phone & account number) with you *at home*. It is also helpful to keep a company directory with executives' home numbers at home in case he asks.

Keep his cell phone or beeper on the charger while in the office and keep these telephone numbers with you at home, including their repair numbers.

If mail needs to be delivered to his house, you might use a courier, limo, company delivery person or a business associate who lives nearby him. If you end up dropping it off, don't forget your mileage expense along with the overtime, if appropriate. If he's not home when the delivery is made, plan in advance with him where you will leave the material (mailbox, behind screen door, under porch mat, back door, etc.) Be sure to tell another delivery person the same locations.

Sleep well tonight!

14
The Dreaded Moving Day

...Across the hall or across town

THE TIME WILL come in your secretarial career when the boss announces you are both moving to a new location. The more dynamic and upwardly mobile he is, the more he moves.

If you pick a day to move, do it on a Friday. Finish packing Friday morning and move in the afternoon. This gives you the weekend, on overtime (if company policy allows) and in casual clothes to go to the new location and get both you and the boss ready for Monday morning. Get necessary authorization or company badges, if required, for the weekend work at the new place.

Things NOT to pack, but carry with you are your calendars, Rolodex, company telephone list or book and a steno pad to jot things down or take action items from the boss.

The last things to pack should be your desk and PC or laptop since you will be using these essentials up until the movers come.

If possible, plan a meeting or vacation day for your boss on move day to keep him out of the confusion...and your way.

Publish advance land-line telephone and mobile phone numbers, fax numbers, addresses, room numbers, etc. if they are different. New business cards and stationery should be ordered well in advance of the move. Notify mail rooms at old and new locations, if applicable, personnel departments, company credit card companies, newspapers and periodicals of the move.

The best move is an organized move. The objective should be to PACK BY DRAWERS so that no re-filing is necessary. Label every box by content and room location at the new office. Mark the boxes whether they are *yours* or the *boss's* and the desk drawer or file cabinet drawer they came out of which will be the drawer numbers they go into. Identical number or name stickers on the boxes and desk drawers save time. Just match the box with the drawer before unpacking.

Notify both the old and new location building management staffs that you are moving *out* and *in* on a certain date and approximate times so they can anticipate the inevitable transition chaos. Most often they are already involved in the move.

For the first week at the new location, give both the old and new receptionist, if applicable, a copy of both your schedules and telephone numbers so they will know where and how to contact you.

Put the new telephone and fax numbers and the new location (including new ZIP code) in all calendars, address books and electronic organizers. Don't forget room numbers and organization codes, if applicable. Also give this information to spouses and key contacts.

Notify clients, customers and other business and personal associates well in advance of the move by either official company notification, email, fax or a personal call. Then follow up with a "We've Moved" card, email or fax containing the new contact information.

Inform your "webmaster" of new contact information for company or personal website and other social media such as Facebook, Linked In, Twitter, Google, etc.

Also plan on coming in much earlier the week before and after the move in case you need to resolve a crisis before the boss gets in. Tell him why this is a good idea and see if it's eligible for overtime pay or personal comp time.

Don't assume the move will go smoothly. Remember old Mr. Murphy and his Law from an earlier chapter? Anticipate what may possibly go wrong and make advance contingency plans. Your office movers may have some suggestions of things to do, or not do, to make things run smoother.

Visit the new location *in advance* of the move and meet the building manager, receptionist, telephone operator, and others working in proximity to your new office. *Get their names and telephone numbers in advance.* Find out building hours, security requirements, parking regulations, cafeteria hours, coffee locations, etc. and publish this information to your organization *before* the move. This way you will see friendly faces on move day and your coworkers will feel somewhat more comfortable when first moving in.

After the new location visit you should have a good idea of what's there now and what's needed in advance of the move (furniture, repairs, painting, etc.). Most people at the new location will accommodate your visit even if the rooms are currently occupied. Visit at least a MONTH BEFORE, at a minimum.

Make a trial run from your home to learn the new route as well as the commuting and parking time. Get parking permits or stickers for you and your boss or organization in advance of the move.

Update new organization charts and telephone directory listings. Distribute maps to the new location, if needed.

Notify travel agents, limo companies, DHL, UPS, Federal Express, the U.S. Post Office and mail room of both the old and the new address and reach numbers. Also alert other service companies so they can update their records and show up at the right place the first time.

Purge the files beforehand! Clean out, shred or archive old files well in advance of the move. Give the boss a list of files so you *both* can sit down together or do individually and decide what to do with certain files. Retain those files required by company or IRS policies.

If the boss wants to throw anything away, have him do it *through you* so you will know where it went. "House clean" several weeks or months before the move date.

Use the company move coordinator or a moving company planner to their fullest extent. They are professionals and will have checklists and "countdown to moving day" suggestions.

Have personnel and medical records for those moving transferred to the new location, if applicable.

You may want to hire temporary help on the Friday before the actual move day and the following Monday to assist you in packing, unpacking or answering phones. Plan this in advance and be aware of the skills you will need as the rates may vary.

Save an empty box to carry the last minute things you and the boss were working on just before the move. This would be the first box to unpack at the new location on Monday or the weekend if you come in. If you have a removable desk drawer tray (plastic compartmentalized small item storage tray) don't dump it into a box or envelope. Place it between two large manila folders, or cardboard, and use rubber bands or tape to secure it. Simply unwrap at the new location and place it back in the desk. This way everything stays neat and in place. *Some movers allow the desks and file cabinets to remain full during the move*, although I've never been this lucky!

Just before you leave the old office for the last time, pull out the little name strips from yours and the boss's multi-button phones (if numbers and system stays the same) so you won't have to remember who was programmed where on your phone. We all become "creatures of habit" and this will save time since you won't have to learn a new setup. Also take door and desk nameplates.

On the Monday morning (or weekday after the move) try to have the boss operate out of a conference room or another empty office until you get his office fully set up.

The boss will want to know where the bathrooms, vending machines, cafeteria or break room and his boss's office are in the new location. Make a list of nearby restaurants. Anticipate this and prepare a list of these locations you know he and his team members will ask about.

Be careful of your back! You shouldn't have to lift heavy boxes, climb on dangerous chairs or take chances with your health during an office move. The boss and the company can't afford to lose you to injury. Hire or get necessary help. He will agree!

Moves are disruptive to both business and people and, for a few days, there can be chaos and mass inefficiencies if the proper guidelines are not followed.

In my career, I've moved eighteen times. Some from one floor to another, some around the corner and some to a new building location in a nearby town. All have not been easy moves, but one thing is certain...you learn something new each time.

A move across the hall, across town or across the nation needs the same amount of organization and preparation in order to be successful and run smoothly.

See the MOVING CHECKLIST on the next page.

Best of luck with *your* move!

MOVING CHECKLIST

( ) Name of move coordinator supervisor / moving company with phone numbers
( ) Telephone / fax / computer set-up ordered / mail address changed
( ) If moving yourself, order boxes, bubble wrap, tape, etc.
( ) New office painted / cleaned / repairs ordered
( ) New stationery ordered
       Business cards
       Buck slips or message pads
       Letterhead & envelopes
       Office nameplates, if a different size

( ) New ID badges / parking permits
( ) Files packed / archived / destroyed
( ) Desks packed
( ) Organization notice changes
( ) Pictures removed / hung at new location
( ) Turn in old desk, file and office keys. Get new ones.
( ) _____
( ) _____
( ) _____
( ) _____

HINTS: Wrap all breakables in bubble wrap or paper, secure with tape and label "Breakable" or "Do not stack on top".

If you start packing a few weeks before the move, don't make the mistake of packing files IN USE too early. Pack old files you need to keep, but don't use... *first*. Have a file list sheet taped on the *side* of the box in case you have to retrieve one.

15
Being Professional

...Not a myth, but *YOUR* career!

MANY LOOK AT the secretarial or AA role as an entrance level position in a business or corporation while others see it as a career for their working life. A good secretary or AA has both upward and lateral mobility and will have to decide on a career path at some point. Whichever path you choose requires preparation for the next level through training, self-development and promotion of your abilities to your boss or supervisor.

Most bosses will welcome your interest in improving yourself. Your skills reflect on his judgment and you should be considered an asset on his balance sheet. Most companies today have a tuition reimbursement program which allows you to start, finish or take graduate college courses through evening, weekend and online courses. Additionally, seminars and in-house training courses improve your product or service knowledge.

No matter at what stage in your career, you should avail yourself of every opportunity to learn as much as you can through these offerings. Make sure all training is documented in your personnel record for appraisals.

Check first to see if your company has a training or development organization from which to select both internal and external training courses. If not, then select courses from local adult educations courses at community colleges, universities, professional secretarial organizations or online self-improvement programs. Then present these to your boss for approval and reimbursement procedures.

If there is any hesitancy on the boss's part to approve these personal development requests, then you need to schedule some time with him to discuss your career and self-improvement goals.

Of course, any company paid training should relate directly or indirectly to your job responsibilities or future career plans. Good starter courses would be time management, organizational skills, assertiveness training, negotiation and computer skills or "Dress for Success" programs. (HINT - Always dress for your next level position. People will already "see" you there). Also, it doesn't hurt to take recurrent training in these fields and skills, as necessary.

Professional organizations or clubs can be very helpful in keeping up with the latest trends in your industry or general business environment. If one is not available, start a local chapter of a national organization or organize a local group who could share secretarial interests. A lot of companies pay the annual dues.

I held quarterly business luncheons with all the secretaries in my organization to discuss new policies and ways to solve old problems which created a sense of camaraderie among the professional staff. My boss liked the idea so much and was so strongly supportive, he picked up the lunch tab.

There is nothing wrong with promoting yourself, your skills, your accomplishments and even your career aspirations to your boss, if properly done. The most appropriate time seems to be at appraisal time each year. Some bosses prefer an interactive appraisal method whereby both of you write your appraisal and then compare them to determine similarities or differences before finalization. Other bosses write the appraisal themselves without any input from you while a few bosses write no appraisals or don't give any feedback. This is very unfair to *you*.

Whichever methods your company or supervisor uses, you should have the right to judge yourself from your own perspective. If the latter is the case, then make it a point to write a letter or orally tell the boss what you accomplished or how you improved during the year. This should be done right before the appraisal process or pay raise time.

I kept what is called a "kudos file" on myself during the year containing complimentary notes or letters, training certificates, honorable mentions, special projects, individual efforts, etc. which showed my progression in the job. It's amazing how much we forget what we've done by the end of the year.

I used this file to help write my own appraisal view for comparison with my boss's view of my performance. He admitted he had forgotten some of the little special projects and tasks he had assigned me and had done well. Don't exaggerate your achievement, but don't take for granted that he will remember everything you did for him during the year.

Keep the boss informed of your career plans or aspirations as he will be the most likely to help you achieve your objectives. If you want to move to another part of the company or be considered for promotion to a staff position, then tell him. All bosses talk among themselves about subordinates, good secretaries, AAs and they can often "make deals" for personnel swaps or promotions.

By the same token, if you are happy in your current position and want to remain a secretary or AA, it is equally important to let the boss know this too. A boss feels more secure and productive knowing he has a loyal and happy employee.

16
Odds & Ends

...Other situations that arise

...Working with an EA

THIS SECTION COVERS a variety of subjects and tips that may be helpful in your daily routine. It doesn't matter if you're a one secretary office or one of many in a secretarial pool of a large corporation. The principles of good secretarial skills transfer to any size business.

WORKING WITH AN EXECUTIVE ASSISTANT (EA) - Although this job title and job function are found more often in larger companies and corporations, this person might also be an assistant manager, "advisor" or "consultant" to the boss. They often are younger, upwardly mobile managers on a "fast track" for promotion or they can be highly paid "gofers" or "hatchet men". Their roles usually involve: representing or "acting for" the boss at meetings, interfacing with customers or clients, responding to the boss's mail, telephone messages and inbox, handling unpleasant issues, and other staff or personnel issues.

If your boss is the top person in your company or large practice, you may find yourself working closely with an EA who may or may not be a long-term fixture in your organization, depending on his career track. Some EAs feel *you* work for them, which may be partially true at times. If there is a "power" conflict or job function issue, it needs to be resolved with your boss immediately for continued harmony in your working relationships.

You should inform the EA about everything going on in the organization, but a seasoned secretary will know what items *do not* get seen by the EA, e.g. boss's salary and other sensitive items. You should use the EA to "defuse" potentially serious problems or situations that you may not be able to resolve yourself. Help the EA to network with the right people who can help and inform him if he's on the right or wrong track to a solution.

Experience will tell you what mail and messages need to be referred to an EA for action and what items can be handled by him and then go to the boss for approval or signature. The EA can be a confidant to you and a "mouthpiece" to the boss on issues you may not want to discuss yourself such as pay raises or other personnel conflicts.

Working together, hand-in-hand so to speak, the secretary and EA complement each other nicely. They need each other's skills to satisfy the boss's demands in the business. I still have fond memories of the great EAs I worked with. We made an excellent synergistic team for the boss.

However, as mentioned before, there must be trust and a clear understanding of each other's roles and responsibilities in order to have a smooth, functioning team. The secretary and

EA relationship should be non-competitive in nature. Without these, power struggles and hard feelings could develop.

VACATION AND DAYS OFF - The boss will usually encourage you to take your deserved vacation time if you leave him well covered with a competent replacement. If you must carry over vacation days into the next year, have it approved in writing by the boss even if there is no formal procedure for this. It protects your days in the event: 1) You move to another job or location or 2) your boss changes jobs or locations and you don't move with him. Now you have irrefutable documentation you were authorized to carry over vacation or comp time. A lot of companies have policies that you must use these carryover days within the first quarter of the following year or lose them. However, this is often negotiable.

Keep track of days taken (vacation, carryover days, personal days, floating holidays and sick time, if optional) throughout the year so if you are asked how many days you have taken, or have left, the answer is at your fingertips. Give the boss quarterly updates of days taken and days left for his vacation planning and coverage requirements.

SUBSTITUTES AND "TEMPS" - Don't assume that your substitute will be trained for your job. Have the person work your last full day with you to see that everything will go smoothly or earlier if required. Try to have the same person for the entire time you are out to ensure continuity with the boss. Give the temp *more* information about the job rather than less and have written procedures in place.

Put encouraging notes in the tickle file like "Day 1 - You're doing great!", etc. On the last day of their assignment, a note like "Thanks so much for helping out" will be greatly appreciated and make them want to work with you again in the future.

When you need temporary help, ask for recommendations from the other secretaries. Not only will they recommend someone or a good temp agency, they will often say who *not* to get or what agency *not* to use. Their opinion will help maintain efficiency and productivity in the office.

FAX, SCANNERS & E-MAIL - Instant communications is the byword of business today and the modern secretary uses these technologies to facilitate business correspondence and communications in an efficient manner. Many of today's office "all-in-one" machines contain a color copier and printer, scanner, fax and both wireless operation from desktops, laptops and smart phones.

FAX - Most fax machines today use standard 20 lb. plain paper, but some less expensive older models still use the flimsy thermal papers.

If re-faxing thermal paper, make a copy on plain paper first to avoid machine jams.

If receiving a fax, check to see if all pages have been received and are legible.

When sending a fax, have a cover sheet and number pages 1 of 6, for example.

Assign responsibility for checking the fax machine and sorting messages.

Check the machine often for enough paper, especially at night. The fax won't tell the sender it is out of paper and may or may not send the correct receipt confirmation.

Most fax machines are not "secure" from prying eyes. Don't send anything that might cause embarrassment if it got in the wrong hands. If you need better security, most models will store incoming faxes in memory until you "unlock" it with a security code.

To be absolutely, positively sure that an important fax is received requires more than one call: 1) Call to say an important fax is coming 2) the fax call itself and 3) a call to the receiver to confirm the fax is received and legible. It's slightly more trouble, but is necessary when sending proprietary or sensitive material.

If you're missing a hotel receipt or invoice, have them fax or email a copy to save time over "snail mail".

SCANNERS & E-MAIL - Scanners are wonderful for duplicating written correspondence, graphs, pictures, blueprint sections and other documents. It basically scans the document and creates a file that can be emailed to the recipient.

Remember, E-mails are *forever* so treat them as such! You can't retrieve them to erase them so use good judgment as to what you say on the keyboard knowing they will always be around somewhere on the Internet, in someone's file or up in the "Cloud". These can come back to "bite" you or the boss and should be carefully reviewed before you hit the "Send" key.

If emails are to be retained, either hard paper copies or a digital filing system is required. To eliminate the paper, set up file categories within the email system and "move" these emails to that file. BACKUP THESE FILES OFTEN either with flash drives or an outside data bank or in the Cloud. I used several different data preservation techniques in case the building caught on fire.

SOCIAL MEDIA IS FOREVER TOO! If you or your boss use Facebook, Twitter, Pinterest, Linked-In, Google, etc., just remember the data *never* disappears once sent. Again, good judgment and discretion are needed to avoid embarrassment and possible disciplinary action, or even termination, by your boss or company policy. Misuse of emails and social media are evident in the news every day, even by high government officials. Please be discrete and use these wonderful tools in a constructive and productive manner.

SNOOPY PEOPLE - Every office has at least one "snoop" and he, or she, may be the root of the infamous office gossip grapevine. To minimize the wrongful use of information:

Make sure your desk and files are locked when you're not in the vicinity. Clear your desk of all proprietary or sensitive material before you leave. Many companies have strict security measures and violating them can be grounds for suspension or dismissal, especially with misuse of government business.

Don't give out copies of the boss's memos without clearing it with him first, even to those who report directly to him. It might contain private, personnel or other information not to be seen by them.

Don't allow others to "look through a file" or "look over your shoulder" to find an item. YOU DO IT! There may be extremely sensitive information in that file and, if disclosed, *you* are responsible.

Snoopy people tend to be very friendly, seemingly trustworthy types. Be cautious about divulging *any* information which may compromise that "trust bond" between you and your boss.

Watch what you say at your desk within "earshot" of others.

Be wary of leaving information on your computer screen when you go on break or to lunch. Also, don't leave sensitive messages on your telephone or answering machine overnight.

If you believe that office security has been breached, report it immediately to your boss. Industrial espionage is a real danger and menace in today's competitive business environment.

TRAVELING BOSSES LOSE THINGS! - Make FIVE copies of his passport (cover, number, visa page), driver's license, airline club cards, frequent flyer cards, credit cards and health insurance cards (all on one sheet of paper, front and back). One copy is for his wallet, one for his briefcase, one for your office copy, one for *your* home copy and one for his spouse. Also make a copy of his airline or train ticket.

BOSS CALLS IN FOR MESSAGES - When you give him the message, put a date and time on it and a check mark to show you have relayed the message, but don't throw it away. Just because you gave him the message doesn't mean he returned the call or took appropriate action. Place the "received" messages on his desk for when he returns and let *him* toss away these "gentle" reminders.

VISITORS TO SEE THE BOSS should be warmly received and offered refreshments, if appropriate. When meeting someone new at your desk, stand and offer your hand and repeat their name to help you remember it. When meeting visitors in the lobby or reception area, extend your hand and introduce yourself first. If the visitor has to wait awhile, you may indicate the location of the bathroom or water fountain.

Be sure the visitor is not "wandering" while waiting for the boss. If he strolls too near the boss's open office door, you may want to close it to prevent conversations from being overheard. After the visitor leaves, ask the boss for the person's business card to either reproduce it for the file or staple it in the Rolodex.

END OF YEAR BUSINESS - You may want to check with the boss's lawyer or accountant to see if you need to keep records of any relevant information in the *following* year for his tax purposes (car mileage, commuting expenses in excess of home to office to home, days out of the state or country, etc.). It is much easier to track this on a daily or weekly basis rather than trying to reconstruct the entire year in December or by April 15th.

STARTING THE NEW YEAR - On the next page is a suggested cleanup checklist to use when starting a new year. I have noted some of the things I did and have left room for you to add others which pertain to your particular office situation.

END OF YEAR CLEANUP CHECKLIST

Start the new year organized!

( )   Close down present year files.
( )   Set up new files: Attendance, Expense vouchers, Invoices, etc.
( )   Copy next year meetings on new calendars.
( )   Store or archive files that need to be retained.
( )   Update electronic contact files or Rolodex, as needed.
( )   Get carryover vacation or comp time approved. File in your personnel file.
( )   Update organization chart and company directory.
( )   Copy birthdays, anniversaries, etc. into new desk & pocket calendars.
( )   Check greeting card reserve stock (birthday, get well, sympathy, congratulation, etc.). Purchase more, if necessary.
( )   Check general office supplies. Reorder as needed. Have a few extra sets of "month" dividers for the new year to use for correspondence, records, etc.
( )   File incoming holiday cards, or a list of them, in next year's October "bring up" file so you know who sent cards the previous year.
( )   Vaccination Records copied if foreign travel expected.
( )   _____
( )   _____
( )   _____
( )   _____
( )   _____

17
"We've Come a Long Way, Baby"

...Past, Present and Future

THIS PARAPHRASE OF a Virginia Slims commercial does indeed highlight the progress women's rights in the business world have made in recent years. For a birthday several years ago, I gave my husband an original copy of *The New York Times* newspaper dated his birth date in December, 1941. We looked in the classified ads section under "Help Wanted" and found these ads for executive secretaries, stenographers and receptionists:

> "Executive secretary to President of large company. Must be attractive with good skills. $100 month start. State age, religion, references. Reply..."
>
> "Stenographer with accounting background. Attractive. $18-23 wk start. Give age, religion, qualifications..."
>
> "Receptionist / secretary. Must be pretty and alert. $20 week start. State age, religion, references..."

The classified section ran *two full columns* of these ads. Can you imagine the legal and social furor they would cause today? Yes, maybe we've come a long way in over 75 years towards equality in the workplace since those ads, but there are still ugly stigmas in our profession which are problematic even today... sexual harassment and discrimination.

The scope and purpose of this book does not allow an in-depth examination of these critical problems. I only point them out so you know there are resources available if your rights are being violated or infringed upon. There are many books and articles on the subjects, but each person's situation is very delicate and very individual. However, you should know your rights are protected by Federal and State laws as well as workplace codes and ethical conduct policies by most employers.

If you are unable to resolve differences through open communication or establishment of mutual ground rules, then you may need to seek advice and a course of action through your personnel organization, an attorney or a Federal or State organization. Your rights as a professional secretary or administrative assistant *are* protected and can be enforced if need be.

The future will bring more awareness, legislation and resolution of these problems as well as more equality in compensation and responsibility for the profession. Technology will only enhance our capabilities, not replace us, so we can provide a more meaningful role for *The Boss Behind The Boss* in the future.

Just a reminder:

> *Remember to have fun!* For the amount of time you spend at your job, you need to enjoy it.

Good luck!

About the author...

Lynne's career spanned thirty years with one company, AT&T in Basking Ridge, NJ although she worked in several divisions such as Bell Laboratories, AT&T International, Marketing and Network Operations at different facility locations in New Jersey.

She lives in the beautiful Blue Ridge Mountains of western North Carolina with her husband, David, and three wonderfully crazy cats. David has also written a spy thriller series of six novels featuring NSA Agent Jon Deats.

The Boss Behind The Boss is available both as a paperback or eBook on **Amazon.com**.

www.ingramcontent.com/pod-product-compliance
Lightning Source LLC
Chambersburg PA
CBHW020928180526
45163CB00007B/2928